Christians and Cultural Difference

CALVIN SHORTS

A series published by the Calvin College Press

Christians and Cultural Difference

by David I. Smith and
Pennylyn Dykstra-Pruim

COLLEGE

Grand Rapids, MI • calvincollegepress.com

Published 2016 by the Calvin College Press
3201 Burton St. SE
Grand Rapids, MI 49546

Publisher's Cataloging-in-Publication data
Names: Smith, David I., author | Dykstra-Pruim, Pennylyn, author.
Title: Christians and cultural difference / David I. Smith ; Pennylyn Dykstra-Pruim.
Description: Grand Rapids [Michigan] : The Calvin College Press, 2016 | Includes bibliographical references.
Series: Calvin Shorts.
Identifiers: ISBN 978-1-937555-15-3 | ISBN 978-1-937555-16-0 (ebook) LCCN 2015945268
Subjects: LCSH Multiculturalism--Religious aspects--Christianity. | Race relations--Religious aspects--Christianity. | Ethnicity--Religious aspects--Christianity. | BISAC RELIGION / Christian Church / General | CULTURAL HERITAGE / Multicultural.
Classification: LCC BV10.2 .S65 2016 | DDC 264--dc23

Scripture quotations, unless otherwise noted are taken from the HOLY BIBLE, TODAY'S NEW INTERNATIONAL VERSION®. TNIV®. Copyright © 2001, 2005 by International Bible Society. Used by permission of Zondervan. All rights reserved worldwide.

Cover design: Robert Alderink
Interior design and typeset: Katherine Lloyd, The DESK

Calvin College Press has no responsibility for the persistence or accuracy of URLs for external or third-party Internet Web sites referred to in this publication and does not guarantee that any content on such Web sites is, or will remain, accurate or appropriate.

Contents

Series Editor's Foreword

Midway along the journey of our life
I woke to find myself in some dark woods,
For I had wandered off from the straight path.

So begins *The Divine Comedy*, a classic meditation on the Christian life, written by Dante Alighieri in the fourteenth century.

Dante's three images—a journey, a dark forest, and a perplexed pilgrim—still feel familiar today, don't they?

We can readily imagine our own lives as a series of journeys, not just the big journey from birth to death, but also all the little trips from home to school, from school to job, from place to place, from old friends to new. In fact, we often feel we are simultaneously on multiple journeys that tug us in diverse and sometimes opposing directions. We recognize those dark woods from fairy tales and nightmares and the all-too-real conundrums that crowd our everyday lives. No wonder we frequently feel perplexed. We wake up shaking our heads, unsure if we know how to live wisely today or tomorrow or next week.

This series has in mind just such perplexed pilgrims.

Each book invites you, the reader, to walk alongside experienced guides who will help you understand the contours of the road as well as the surrounding landscape. They will cut back the underbrush, untangle myths and misconceptions, and suggest ways to move forward.

And they will do it in books intended to be read in an evening or during a flight. Calvin Shorts are designed not just for perplexed pilgrims, but also for busy ones. We live in a complex and changing world. We need nimble ways to acquire knowledge, skills, and wisdom. These books are one way to meet those needs.

John Calvin, after whom this series is named, recognized our pilgrim condition. "We are always on the road," he said, and although this road, this life, is full of perplexities, it is also "a gift of divine kindness which is not to be refused." Calvin Shorts takes as its starting point this claim that we are called to live well in a world that is both gift and challenge.

In *The Divine Comedy*, Dante's guide is Virgil, a wise but not omniscient mentor. So too, the authors in the Calvin Shorts series don't pretend to know it all. They, like you and me, are pilgrims. And they invite us to walk with them as together we seek to live more faithfully in this world that belongs to God.

Susan M. Felch
Executive Editor
The Calvin College Press

Additional Resources

Additional online resources for *Christians and Cultural Difference* may be available at http://calvincollegepress. com/.

Additional information, references, and citations are included in the notes at the end of this book. Rather than using footnote numbers, these comments are keyed to phrases and page numbers.

What is Culture?

Imagine yourself standing on a hilltop overlooking a lush valley, pristine and full of promise. A stream winds through groves of maples. Cicadas and birds fill the breezes with song. You decide to stay, stacking fallen branches for shelter and clearing a plot of land where selected herbs and vegetables will now grow in patterns of your own design. You have cultivated your surroundings. Future visitors will see that there is more here than just landscape; there are signs of human activity, planning, and living. In other words, they will find evidence of human culture.

As you settle in your valley and are joined by others, the first changes you made to the land begin to affect what you do. Having gone to the trouble to establish a place for vegetables to grow, you stay nearby to tend it. You become attached to your particular spot and feel anxious if it seems threatened. You find pliable reeds near the stream and soon learn to weave baskets instead of using animal-skin bags. The emerging community develops routines and adapts them to the natural cycles of this environment. Your neighbors learn to interpret a nod to the left, or a waggle of the fingers, in a particular way. You find new fruits and animals and give them names. You develop turns of phrase and shared gestures that soon make you harder to understand for anyone from a different place.

It is not long before your culture-making has made

you and those in your valley something different from the generically human. Together you have begun to develop particular cultural patterns tied to your shared experiences. Your habits, your tastes, your gestures, your stories, even your brain have become shaped a little differently. These patterns form the culture of your valley.

In our description of your budding valley community, we have already used the word *culture* several times. One of the problems in talking about *culture* is that we use the word in different ways. Often we talk about, say, Chinese culture in a way that suggests all Chinese live in China and they all share the same behaviors and outlook. In the next breath we talk about youth culture as opposed to adult culture, focusing on age rather than a political border to define a culture. We hear about corporate culture or black culture or Islamic culture; suddenly culture seems tied to organizations or race or religion. At other times we consider culture an elite achievement, making a distinction between high culture and low culture or between the cultured and the uncultured; now the ability to appreciate Bach, Cervantes, or Monzaemon is the dividing line.

It may surprise us to find that the word *culture* originally meant tilling the land. It is related to the word *agriculture*. Culture, in the sense most relevant to this book, refers to the human activity of transforming our surroundings and making patterns, products, and ways of seeing that in turn shape our sense of self. Culture, in this sense, is not the possession of the few; everyone participates just by being human, whether the patterns have to do with carrots or concertos.

In our imagined valley, we are still closer to carrots than concertos, but as you learn to survive and then to thrive, your community develops patterns that give order to your existence. Based on what has worked well, these patterns become reassuring and keep chaos at bay. In time, they feel like the way things always have been and seem like the way things should be. At the same time, people over in the next valley have been working out their own patterns. One day you encounter someone from that other valley, and find yourself both curious and afraid. You hear unfamiliar words, conversation is awkward, you notice behaviors that you fear may be hostile—but you can't tell for sure. You are uncertain how to interpret what you see, and you are not sure what motives are in play. You have encountered cultural difference.

We have various ways of talking about cultural differences. When the focus is on how different cultural groups can live together in the same social or political space, we talk of "multicultural" matters. When people travel to foreign places and learn to get around, we tend to speak of "cross-cultural" journeys. These are both important, but the focus of this book is on a third term. When we begin to interact with someone whose cultural formation is different from ours, whether at the ends of the earth, in the next valley, or on our own street, and when we attempt to understand one another well, we are involved in "intercultural" interaction. *Intercultural* describes what happens *between* cultures. Intercultural learning happens when we learn from one another as our lives intersect. Our focus in this book is why intercultural learning matters, and in particular why it is important for Christians.

THEMES OF THIS BOOK

The book addresses three broad themes. In Chapter Two, we focus on identity. We connect cultural *identity* to the image of God, sin, and redemption. Does the creation of humans in God's image mean we are all really the same? Does celebrating difference ignore evil? What difference does it make to my identity if I call myself *Christian*? Chapter Four considers *mission* and the ways we reach out to others. How does cultural difference complicate outreach? How can the life of Jesus serve as a model? Chapter Six turns to *ethics*, and in particular an ethic of hospitality to others. How is the practice of hospitality in our homes and neighborhoods related to bigger issues of cultural difference? What is the place of kindness to strangers in the Christian life? In Chapter Seven, we explore some strategies for engaging with cultural differences in gracious ways, before concluding in the final chapter with some words of encouragement.

Those with sharp eyes will have noticed some numbers missing. Chapters Three and Five explore some slightly more extended examples of what we talk about in the other chapters. We hope they will help to spark reflection.

This book, and the series in which it belongs, aims to keep things short and simple. There is a wealth of further literature out there for those who want to dig a little deeper. This book offers perspectives from two Christians: one white, male, and of British origin (the "I" of Chapters 1-4) and one Asian, female, and raised mostly in the USA (the "I" of Chapters 5-8). It cannot speak for everyone. But we hope that this little book can offer food for thought and some nudges toward living more faithfully with cultural difference.

2

Culture and Who We Are

Ancient Greece split the world into Greeks and *barbarians*, meaning babblers who can't speak properly. Natives of Papua New Guinea suspected at first that the pale World War II soldiers who descended from the sky and had removable second skins must be sky spirits rather than human beings like themselves. Recent history continues to produce modern day conflicts, slavery, and genocide in which certain cultural groups are treated as subhuman. Throughout history and around the world, we have been tempted to think of members of other cultural groups as not quite human. Our sense of our own identity is shaped by our culture, and so is our sense of the identity of others.

IMAGES OF GOD

Ancient Near Eastern cultures saw their rulers as "images" or representatives of their gods. Common folk, foreigners, and enemies need not apply; it was *kings* who were the divine image. Genesis 1 presents a different scenario. All human beings, male and female, are made in the image of God (Genesis 1:26-28). All have dignity and value. Each stands under God's promise to seek an accounting if their life is harmed (Genesis 9:5-6). The "image of God" theme in Scripture offers a reason to honor the worth of other human beings, regardless of how much they do or don't resemble us.

This might seem to cut short our interest in cultural differences. After all, if everyone is made in God's image, doesn't that mean that deep down everyone is basically the same? Should we just emphasize what is universally shared and not focus on cultural identities? Underneath our surface differences, isn't it our common humanness that counts?

It's not quite that simple. Part of what makes us human, part of what is shared, is our ability and calling to shape culture. The image of God is explained in Genesis 1 in terms of ruling:

> Then God said, "Let us make human beings in our image, in our likeness, so that they may rule over the fish in the sea and the birds in the sky, over the livestock and all the wild animals, and over all the creatures that move along the ground." (Genesis 1:26)

Ruling was part of what it meant to be a god's image in the ancient world. But in Genesis, it is *all* humans who are called to rule and to help shape the world. A little later, we see Adam tending the garden and making up names for the animals; God's human image begins to shape culture.

In modern times, this idea of dominion over the world has been linked with selfish abuse of the environment, but the rule imagined in Genesis is to resemble God's rule.

Authority in the image of God, who is love, will involve care, sustenance, and delight. Proverbs 8 pictures God's Wisdom taking joy in creation:

> I was filled with delight day after day,
> rejoicing always in his presence,
> rejoicing in his whole world
> and delighting in humankind.
> (Proverbs 8:30-31)

Wise culture building happens when we shape our surroundings by crafting tools, words, dwellings, images, and practices that enable delight in God, delight in creation, and delight in other people. Then we reflect our creation in God's image. As we do so, through our culture-crafting we become different from those working in other times and places.

There are basic shared human characteristics and experiences, but people express and inhabit them differently in different cultures. Joy, sadness, fear, anger, and love seem to be experienced by people everywhere, but if I were to bring my wife a slain tapir, it might be a less successful act of love than in some other places. A recent study of the automatic brain responses of Americans and Japanese found that, when shown images of fearful faces, participants reacted more quickly and powerfully to faces from their own culture. They identified more quickly with fear when they saw it on faces that looked more similar to their own. Cultural differences become quite deeply inscribed in who we are and how we see the world.

Cultural differences, which grow out of our shaping of the world, are part of what it means to be human, made in God's image, yet they easily become grounds for rejecting others. Judging others simply for being culturally different suggests that we want to keep the image of God for ourselves, for our own group, as if only we have the right to shape culture. Honoring everyone as made in God's image allows us to honor the responses of others to their human calling. As Dietrich Bonhoeffer puts it:

> God did not make others as I would have made them. God did not give them to me so that I could dominate and control them, but so that I might find the Creator by means of them. Now other people, in the freedom with which they were created, become an occasion for me to rejoice, whereas before they were only a nuisance and a trouble for me. God does not want me to mold others into the image that seems good to me, that is, into my own image. Instead, in their freedom from me, God made other people in God's own image.

Others are not made in my image, but in God's image. And if I open myself to those who are different from me, I may glimpse the Creator in the way they image God. Difference, not just sameness, is rooted in the image of God.

BROKEN IMAGES

Of course it would be nice to be able to stop here. But what about evil? Don't we see cultures that foster violence, idolatry, exploitation, greed, promiscuity, hatred, false pride? Doesn't that put a stop to all the optimistic talk of opening ourselves to others? Aren't there things in other cultures that we should be wary of being open to?

The human calling is to shape culture in wise ways. Being made in God's image gives us freedom to help shape the world, but we can use that freedom to distort and destroy, and as we do so, sin becomes bound up with culture. Not all culture is wise. Simple celebration of difference will no longer do, for not all differences are benign. Suspicion might be the right response to some parts of any culture. Cultures are flawed and offer patterns that should be resisted.

Naïve celebration is too simple. And yet automatic suspicion is too simple, too. The mistake does not lie in thinking that other cultures might be flawed—all cultures are. It is to be too quick to find flaws in other cultures while giving ourselves easy credit because our own identity feels closer to the norm. We tend to assume that our own ways have a naturalness about them, and we easily misinterpret difference as sin.

One study tells the story of an older Korean woman visiting the US who was admitted to the hospital. She did not speak English and became agitated when medical staff began immediately to treat her. The staff interpreted her behavior as aggressive, perhaps even psychotic, and sedated her. She was upset that medics younger than her seemed to be acting without her permission, a violation of the right way to act in her culture. The staff were upset that she was not submitting to what they felt was needed treatment, a violation of the right way to act in their context. As happens so often in cultural conflicts, each side was convinced that it was the other who was behaving badly.

Another example: On the second day of a trip to Germany with American college students who had been learning German, one student admitted to a sudden realization. He had been learning German for years in school, he said, but this was the first time he had been to Germany. It suddenly hit him that there were all these people, as he put it, "going about shopping, thinking, arguing, dreaming, chatting over meals, playing games, praying, *in German*, all the time, like this whole other world." He was familiar with a second language as a school subject but was only now fully realizing that his own language and his own daily experience of the world were not normal for most other people. We can know a lot *about* other cultures before this realization really dawns.

Our native language feels like the natural way to speak. The rhythms and ways of our native community often seem natural too, for good and ill. It can feel easier to spot the evils in another culture than those in our own familiar world, or at least to think they are more worrying. Here again we often want to think of ourselves more than others as images of God, helping shape things the right way. Or it can happen the other way around as we idealize another culture while seeing only failures in our own. Ashamed of evils close to home, we imagine others as inherently more noble.

Both reactions have problems, for all are created in God's image, yet "all have sinned and fall short of the glory of God" (Romans 3:23). In all cultures there is evidence of culture-crafting that is wise and culture-crafting that has gone awry. In all cultures there is room for gratitude, glimpses of the Creator, and repentance from life shaped badly. A saying of Jesus about attending first to the beam in our own eye before helping with the speck in another's eye comes to mind (Matthew 7:3-5). Engaging with other cultures may help us along the way to our own needed repentance. Facing the reality of evil in ourselves as well as in the world at large does not mean avoiding intercultural learning; in fact it may invite it.

THE TRUE IMAGE

As we turn to Jesus, the question of our identity expands again.

To be a Christian is to be called to repentance. Christians are called by God out of every tribe and nation and people and tongue to be conformed to the image of Christ. Christians in cultures that are currently powerful are especially tempted to equate their culture with being

Christian, perhaps equating Christian identity with white or middle class or American or European identity. But Christ has more claim over us than do our cultural loyalties. We may need to relinquish, resist, and reshape parts of our cultural identity if we are to avoid being conformed "to the pattern of this world" (Romans 12:2).

We are called as Christians to a new unity not based on our tribal allegiances. In Christ "there is no Gentile or Jew, circumcised or uncircumcised, barbarian, Scythian, slave or free." Instead there are those putting on "compassion, kindness, humility, gentleness and patience" toward one another regardless of their cultural origins (Colossians 3:11-14). In Christ, who is "the image of the invisible God," we are called back to being God's image, a people from every nation, tribe, and tongue in whom the Creator can be glimpsed.

So do we now leave our cultural selves behind? Are we back to saying we are actually all the same deep down? Not really. Paul pictures us as stones being built together into a temple, or as parts of the same body, each different but necessary to make up the whole (1 Corinthians 12:12-27; Ephesians 2:14-22). "Just as a body, though one, has many parts, but all its many parts form one body, so it is with Christ" (1 Corinthians 12:12).

These images describe a church that from the beginning embraced a range of cultures. There was never a time when the Christian church spoke only one language—Jerusalem was made up of both Greek and Aramaic speakers. At Pentecost, people from many cultures were added to the church, and the Spirit of God was heard speaking their various languages rather than endorsing just one (Acts 2:1-12). A short time later we see Jewish Christians praying together with formerly despised Samaritans (Acts 8:14-17). The first conflicts in the church recorded in the book of Acts were around equality of provision for widows from different cultural groups (Acts 6:1). And Peter soon finds himself swallowing his reluctance to eat with Gentiles (Acts 10:9-35).

There are real cultural differences and even hostilities in the background when Christians are described as being made into the body of Christ, the true image of God. This renewed image, like the first image of God, includes cultural difference. Our cultural identities are not erased, but healed. Hostility is laid aside, and the other is embraced. As Andrew Walls puts it:

> The Ephesian metaphors of the temple and of the body show each of the culture-specific segments as necessary to the body but as incomplete in itself. Only in Christ does completion, fullness, dwell. And Christ's completion, as we have seen, comes from all humanity.... None of us can reach Christ's completeness on our own. We need each other's vision to correct, enlarge, and focus our own; only together are we complete in Christ.

In Christ, we find a worth that is not rooted in boasting about ourselves or in despising others. In Christ, our identity is shaped so as to make space for others. Christ has embraced them too, from every culture, and has called them into his body, his temple. They too are made in the image of God, are fallen and in need, and are drawn into the new image of God, the body of Christ. Christian identity and intercultural learning fundamentally belong together. In the next chapter, we will explore an example of this connection.

3

Wisdom at the Well

I had been familiar with the story for decades. Jesus is traveling and stops by a well, asking a Samaritan woman for water. The conversation turns to her need for living water before Jesus brings to light the woman's five past husbands and lack of marriage to her present partner. They end up discussing the proper place to worship, and Jesus says that true worshippers will worship in spirit and truth. You can read the story in John 4.

It's a story that seems made for sermons about evangelism. Jesus meets an unbeliever and deftly turns talk from refreshment to repentance. Yet if you look more closely, the conversation is a little odd. The transition from water to living water is smooth, but then when the woman asks for the living water, she is told "go get your husband." This seems abrupt. Why does Jesus suddenly switch from water to husbands? A few moments later there is another lurch in the conversation. When Jesus points out her history of husbands, the Samaritan woman suddenly wants to talk about which temple is the right place to worship. Again it comes out of the blue. Why the sudden switch?

For years I had a story in my head that made sense of it all. I had heard it in sermons, read it in books, and when I recently pulled Bible commentaries from a library shelf, I found that almost all of them had the same story in mind. It goes like this. The Samaritan woman is a sinner who needs to repent from her immoral past. (*Though not a prostitute ...* one commentator began). Once she seems ready to talk about eternal life, Jesus exposes her sin so that she can confess and believe. (*His obvious wish to reform her life ...* wrote another). This makes her uncomfortable, and she does her best to wriggle out of the spotlight by changing the subject to temples. Better to talk religion than to face exposure and actual repentance.

It was a tidy story, but it became unsettled by an experience of learning from another culture. I came across an account of how some women in Afghanistan read the passage. Their reading shook my confidence that I had it all wrapped up. Before turning to that, let's think for a moment about why I read it the way I did and why Afghan women might read it differently.

Psychologists have studied how people in different cultures explain events—the kinds of causes we instinctively reach for to make sense of things. Westerners tend, on average, to have a stronger preference for internal explanations of behavior. Why did she help me? Because she is a nice person. Because she is kind. Because something good inside her made her do it. Westerners tend to think of themselves as individuals making free choices, and they interpret others through the same lens. Asians (again on average) have a stronger tendency to reach for external explanations. Why did she help me? There was no one else around. She was the nearest person. Something in the situation made her help appropriate. In general,

Asians are more likely to think of themselves as part of a network of obligations and cause-effect sequences that reduce the role of individual choices. Both of these are generalizations—individuals will vary—but they do point to real differences in how we reach for explanations.

And so back to our Samaritan story. I recently ran across this passage in Kate McCord's *In the Land of Blue Burqas*:

> I was often amazed when an Afghan heard a Jesus story for the first time and then told me what it means. Jesus spoke to a woman at a well, a woman who had had several husbands and was not married to her current partner. My Afghan woman friends immediately saw the woman's shame. No woman in Afghanistan can arrange her own marriage. The woman at the well had been used by five men, and the last didn't even have the decency to marry her. The woman's question about where she should worship made sense. With her lack of honor and freedom, she couldn't have gone to Jerusalem or Mount Gerazim to worship. Stunningly, Jesus told her she could worship where she was, told her she was not cut off from God. He said worship isn't about form or place but about spirit and truth. For my Afghan friends … this is good news!

Here was a different story to make sense of the conversational turns. The woman was at the well alone, rather than when the rest of the women came, because of her shame. The many husbands were not her choice, nor was her current status. The situation forced on her had pushed her to the margins. As the conversation turned to eternal life, her inability to join worship came to the front of her mind. Jesus was indeed calling her to faith, but perhaps he was ministering to her shame more than to her sin.

Leave aside for a moment debating the correct interpretation—that matters, but my concern here is different. What struck me as I read was that in decades of reading the biblical passage I had simply never asked myself whether or to what degree the Samaritan woman's relationships were chosen by her. I tend to assume that I can make my own choices about such things, and that they are motivated from within. I tend to interpret others the same way. These are the ways my cultural formation and my life experience incline me to think. Research on cultural difference predicts that I would think this way.

What if this leaves me, as a Western male reader, sitting in judgment on the Samaritan woman in the story while Jesus was freeing her from such judgment? Perhaps I had been seeing her as the rest of her town did, rather than as Jesus did.

Does this leave everything relative, with each person locked in his or her own culture? No. Quite the opposite. It means that the perspectives that arise from my culture may not have a monopoly on truth, and that I need to learn from others to test my own sense of things. Even when I am seeking truth by reading the Scriptures, I can gain from being open to the voices of cultural others.

4

Culture and Reaching Out

little over two hundred years ago, a German watchmaker named Johannes Emde set out on a long journey across cultures. He moved from Germany to Surabaya, Indonesia, where he settled and married a Javanese woman. Soon he began to preach his Christian faith. He asked children to pass out extracts from the Scriptures in the local language at the markets. After a few decades, he had gathered more than thirty converts and became a founder of the Christian churches in that area of Java.

Part of what propelled Emde to Java was puzzlement. He had heard that in Indonesia there was no winter season as there was in Europe. He was perturbed that this seemed to contradict the promise in Genesis 8:22 that "summer and winter … will never cease." He might have questioned whether his own experience was a perfect match for the seasons in the place where Genesis was written. He might have asked himself whether Genesis 8 could be speaking in a particular cultural setting to make a promise to particular people. But it seemed clear to him that the Bible said there had to be summer and winter. He decided to go to Indonesia to investigate for himself.

Emde started out troubled by the idea that his own experiences might not be universal. It is not entirely surprising that in his missionary work, he was suspicious of the ancient Javanese culture. The churches that resulted

41

from his ministry in Indonesia had a European cultural flavor. His converts became known locally as "Dutch Christians."

MISSION AND THE FAITH-CULTURE MIX

Emde's story points to a tension that runs through the history of Christian missions, all the way back to the early church's debate about whether Gentile Christians needed to become Jewish (Acts 15). We experience our faith, our relationship to God, and our attempts to be faithful from inside our own cultural identity. When we reach out to share our faith with others, where is the boundary between sharing our faith and sharing our culture? Do we imply that to become real Jesus followers, others also have to become European, or American, or share our politics, or like our music? Do we imply that a specific kind of cultural identity, local to our time and place, is the key to being properly Christian?

Easy solutions seem tempting. Some might argue that missions should be abandoned—that they are hopelessly bound up with colonialism, arrogance, and the destruction of other cultures. Suspicion of the idea of mission may be justified by real abuses. Past missionaries to Native Americans, for instance, used strategies of forced assimilation, including separating children from their parents and forbidding them to use their native language. Such abuses are rightly condemned. But sharing wisdom among cultures can be helpful to all concerned. All cultures (including our own) are fallen. All contain elements that may need to be challenged. And all may contain admittedly imperfect yet hopeful examples of wise ways of being in the world that deserve wider adoption. Sharing truths interculturally is not necessarily oppressive. The alternative to abusive sharing of the faith need not be silence.

Others might imagine that the solution is to just preach the gospel without imposing any cultural expectations. But it is not that simple. Those who preach the gospel are always coming from somewhere. Our faith cannot be cleanly separated from culture, as if we could strip ourselves of all of our own formation and hold naked faith in one hand and mere culture in the other. The questions we bring to Scripture, the ways we interpret and try to obey, the very words we use and think with are themselves cultural.

I remember the sense of newness I felt when visiting a Bible college in Indonesia and seeing the word *Allah*, the general local word for *God*, displayed prominently on the walls in Bible verses. I also recall a conversation with a British theologian who had taught for some years in Africa. He confessed that it was only when he realized that his theological textbooks had no answers to his students' questions about what to do if you were a convert and had several wives, or if the local shaman had cursed you, that it became clear to him that the textbooks were answering the questions of a particular cultural setting. And conversation with African-American brothers and sisters has helped me begin to see issues needing justice and healing in my own neighborhood to which I might otherwise have remained blind. It is good to try to become aware of our own cultural biases because faith is always understood and expressed within a culture. Separate faith entirely from culture and we would have no words, or questions, or practices in which to articulate it.

There is no magical recipe for disentangling what is just local culture from what needs to be held to and shared more widely. Many of our questions about where the boundaries lie can only be answered piecemeal in actual engagement with others, inside the process of learning about each other. Things that once seemed non-negotiable to us may come to look different after learning with others. Without aiming to solve these questions ahead of time, we here suggest two issues worth thinking about as we wrestle with questions of culture and mission. The first is about where Christianity travels from and to, and the second concerns taking Jesus's life as a model for mission.

MISSION AND THE GEOGRAPHY OF CHRISTIANITY

Some years ago I was chatting with some English-speaking teens about the language programs at their school. When I asked them whether they thought their Spanish learning would be useful to them after leaving school, almost none of them said yes. Surprised, I asked why. "Because I am not going to be a missionary" was the general reply.

More recently I heard some people talking about a mission trip they were planning. They worried aloud about the "darkness" of the country they planned to visit and the idolatry and superstition that they would face as they went out.

Both encounters suggested a view of the world in which the place where "we" (in these cases English-speaking North Americans) live is where the Christian faith is most at home. From here it is taken out to darker, more distant lands. The diversity of language and culture in our own neighborhoods, and the darkness and idolatries of our own culture, are passed over in silence.

A hundred years ago there was some plausibility to the idea that Christianity flowed from cultures rooted in Europe out to other lands. Even then, this story obscured the long histories of Christianity in other parts of the world. Today this idea is even further from reality. Most of the world's Christians are not white, do not speak English, and do not live in the West. There has been an enormous shift in the global pattern of Christian faith, from a time when the Christian heartlands were in Europe and North America to the present, when most Christians are natives of the global south. Western countries are no longer the biggest senders of Christian missionaries. As Andrew Walls puts it, "the most striking feature of Christianity at the beginning of the third millennium is that it is predominantly a non-Western religion."

Change has also come to the West. American and

European cities today are places where people of many ethnicities, cultures, and religions live together, and the Christians living in them are culturally diverse. A few years ago I was driving back to Grand Rapids, Michigan, where I live. I was with the children of some African friends, a Christian refugee family, and we had spent the morning at the beach. They told me that their parents were not at home, and directed me across town to a quiet suburb. We pulled up outside a house, and I could hear music. They led me to the rear of the house, and we opened a gate in a tall fence. As I stood in the gate, behind me were the houses and streets that many would associate with white, Western suburbia. In front of me was an African wedding: drummers, dancers, African dress—a vivid slice of central Africa. If I had not known this family, I might not have known this eruption of African culture was there—and yet my friends were only the most recent additions to a city already home to people of various origins, cultures, and languages.

The world is not divided into Christians who share my culture and foreigners far off with whom I have no connection. Yet some Westerners have a lingering sense that when they reach out to people of other cultures, they are moving culturally from home to a foreign place, from the center to the edge, from the heart of the faith to its boundaries. We should not assume that our cultural home is where God most likes to live. If we are not open to learning from believers of other cultural identities, we are saying that the foot does not need the hand (1 Corinthians 12:14-20), that the image of God has one cultural face.

MISSION AND THE LIFE OF CHRIST

Recent writers about missions have, of course, been aware of past abuses and the changes in the global church and have rightly emphasized humility and flexibility. Christ calls us to humble service and warns against lording it over others. He welcomed those who were shunned by the religious folk and nationalists of his day. The call to imitate Christ offers a contrast with images of mission that are tainted by power and pride. Jesus "did not consider equality with God something to be used to his own advantage; rather, he made himself nothing by taking the nature of a servant" (Philippians 2:6-7). Christ was born into a flesh-and-blood human culture and seeks to indwell all human cultures, living within each of them. Like Christ, we can look for what the Father is doing and seek signs of the work of the Holy Spirit in all human cultures (John 5:17-19; Acts 10). Mission must be framed by discipleship, and the disciples must be like their Master.

In the past few decades, various popular books on missions have taken this idea a step further, suggesting that we should specifically imitate Christ's incarnation as we enter other cultures. Christ was born into first-century Jewish culture and spent years listening and learning before finally beginning his servant ministry; Christians likewise should enter other cultures "incarnationally" as humble learners. The idea that we should be incarnational as we enter another culture is intended to lead us to humble service, but it has also resulted in problems that are reflected in the decline of its use.

Talk of an incarnational approach to another culture implies that we should, as it were, become incarnated into another culture as little children, ready to learn. Some have implied that what Jesus was doing in the incarnation was itself intercultural learning as he acquired Jewish culture so that he could later preach. However, Jesus being born in Israel is not an example of intercultural learning, but of a person growing up in his native culture.

The challenges of cultural difference have to do with how we have already been shaped by our first culture or cultures. We are mismatched with the signals a new culture is sending us, as if we had spent years developing the muscles for distance running and then been asked to join a swimming team. Growing up in our own culture and learning its ways is a somewhat different process than intercultural learning. Being God was not a culture that Jesus had to unlearn to become Jewish. Jesus was growing up as a fully human Jewish male, a member of his own culture, not engaging in intercultural learning. Our challenge when we encounter a new culture is that we have already grown up, we are already culturally shaped. Talk of incarnation has turned out to be an ill-fitting way to describe the challenges of intercultural encounter.

A further risk of using incarnational language—unintended, to be sure, but still present—is that if we think of ourselves entering another culture in the same way that God entered a fallen world to redeem it, we put ourselves in the role of God and the culture we are entering in the role of the fallen world that needs transformation. This does little to encourage reflection on our own sin and need for repentance. Perhaps it is not accidental that when the New Testament writers talk of imitating Christ, they put more emphasis on imitating his cross and resurrection than his incarnation. When we encounter new cultures, we are not gods being born into new worlds to raise them to our level. We are fallen humans dying to self and being raised with Christ as we share God's grace with others who share our condition.

While we should be careful with how we talk about the incarnation in relation to mission, the key emphasis that the idea of incarnational mission was trying to capture remains perfectly valid. As Paul puts it, "In your relationships with one another, have the same attitude of mind Christ Jesus had" (Philippians 2:5). Humility, self-sacrificial service, a refusal to lord it over others—these are all things that we are called to learn from Christ, from his life and death. They are all deeply relevant to how we approach and live among people of other cultures. And they all cut deeply against the temptation to notice the specks in others' eyes before noticing the planks in our own. If we do not examine ourselves on this point, mission too easily becomes condescension and imposition, and we confuse the grace of God with our favorite ways of being human. But when we set pride aside, we find that mission is not saving the world as Jesus did, but rather serving the many different people called to be part of the body of Christ, led by the one Spirit.

5

More than Good Intentions

When my family picked up our Asian exchange student at the airport, there were other Asian faces in the crowd, but we identified him from his Facebook pictures. We had done our homework: trying to get a feel for his family and background and sharing important information about ourselves. We had always said that it would be good for our kids if we hosted an international exchange student. They would have to share space, food, and attention with a stranger. They would get a chance to help another person understand life in Midwest US-America. They would have to live with someone quite different from themselves. Turns out that even though I'm the one who leads workshops on intercultural learning, I had a lot to learn, too.

Minh settled in easily. He shared readily about his family, their Christian faith, and how he ended up studying in Michigan. He made a point to play video games with my youngest, to ask my oldest questions about getting around campus, to play guitar at our church, and to carry my daughter's bags and musical instruments whenever they were out together. This habit was looked on with some skepticism by my rather independent daughter. I reasoned with her that this was Minh's way of being kind, respectful, and caring. From his cultural standpoint, he was probably doing what he felt he should as part of the family. I told her she should let him. She ought to say, "thank you," and she should mean it.

So far so good, until the bathroom issues began. My two boys and Minh shared a bathroom. House rules: you clean the bathroom you use most. So the three boys were in charge of keeping their bathroom tidy and cleaning it with lemony-smelling products. They even had a schedule detailing who was responsible for which fixtures on which weeks. Clear, organized, foolproof.

After a few weeks though, I felt the situation needed a mild intervention. What bugged me was that I would peek in and find the sink and counter area wet. Obviously while brushing teeth, shaving, or whatever else teenage boys do at bathroom sinks, there is a lot of water sloshing. The first few times I simply dried up the counter myself. I casually mentioned it to one son, then the other one. But things did not improve. So I reminded everyone that they should keep their bathroom tidy. I did this in an indirect way, sensitive to the Asian idea of "face" or public esteem, so that no one person felt critiqued in front of others. I brought the issue up more than once in different indirect ways. But it seemed the more I mentioned it, the wetter the boys' counter got.

Fortunately our exchange student had a lot of natural charm in addition to experience living in the US. So he did a lot of things I appreciated, such as bringing his dinner plate to the dishwasher and saying "thank you" after every meal (which forced my children to do the same). Because of his impeccable manners and general good nature, he accumulated a great deal of good will. I also assumed he meant well towards us.

But the wet bathroom annoyed me. Why was this so hard? It wasn't until a while later that I realized one way of tidying up after yourself in a toilet-sink area in some cultures is, in fact, to rinse the area with water. In some countries, there is even a sprayer for this purpose. So the more my exchange student tried to show me he was cleaning up the bathroom, the more I thought I was living with three bathroom water slobs.

We were both trying. We both wanted that bathroom to be clean. We both wanted to have a good exchange experience. But we were both missing something: knowledge about how the other person in his or her culture defined *clean* in the specific context of a bathroom counter.

Good intentions are a great starting point for intercultural relationships. However, we have to go beyond good intentions, because as this simple story shows, they alone are not enough. Whether we are guests, hosts, or on neutral turf interacting with folks in our communities, we need to keep learning and building our understanding of other cultures and of ourselves, so that we have good strategies for figuring out what is going on in our encounters with people who are different from us. We need to learn how to act in ways that are perceived as we intend them to be. It does little good to shower others with kindnesses if those same actions in their culture are in fact insults.

I've learned two important lessons sharing my home with strangers. First, good will alone is not enough. We need to keep learning from the others we live with, in our home or in our world. Learning more about each other gives us new perspectives on how we can better negotiate life together. Second, even if it puzzles you, there is probably a logical reason for why others do what they do. We might not agree with their reasons, but we gain a lot when we try to understand or interpret what's going on from their cultural perspective, taking their motives into account.

Minh and I made it past the bathroom issues because of the good will between us and because, let's face it, a little water on the bathroom counter is not a big deal. But I did not understand or appreciate how hard he was trying to please me until I learned about wet bathrooms in other cultures. Learning more about other cultures made me able to appreciate Minh even more and reminded me that I have to keep working on building my own intercultural skills and understanding.

6

A Bigger Hospitality

When I was five, my family moved to the US. I wanted to fit in. I wanted long hair, not the short mandatory bob-cut of a Taiwanese schoolgirl. I refused to speak Taiwanese. And when Tommy from down the street said his favorite show was *Mr. Rogers' Neighborhood,* I became a fan, too. At the start of each episode, Fred Rogers comes into his house and swaps his shoes for sneakers and his coat for his iconic zipped cardigan as he sings: "Won't you be my neighbor?" In this made-for-children series, three decades of viewers became part of an ideal community. Neighbors would stop by to share a story or watch a video to learn how taffy was made. Mr. Rogers would invite us to welcome a neighbor or explore a shop in town. Viewers imagined together in the Land-of-Make-Believe how someone else might feel about a situation and how they could solve a problem together. This TV neighborhood became the type of place I wanted to fit into—my new ideal neighborhood.

Although I've lived in various cities on four continents, I still haven't found Mr. Rogers' neighborhood. Few neighborhoods look like that TV ideal. Many are marked by segregation. Often neighbors do not know the names of the people who live near their home, let alone stop by to share stories or taffy. What is often missing is that sense of neighborliness or hospitality, both in the traditional sense of welcome, food, and shelter, and in the broader sense of how we relate to each other.

HOSPITALITY AROUND THE WORLD

Traditional hospitality has strong roots in many cultures worldwide. In the Papyrus of Ani, a text from ancient Egypt, a royal explains to the god Osiris that he is worthy of a pleasant afterlife because he has fed and clothed the poor and given shelter to those in need; in short, he has shown hospitality. Offering hospitality is part of other Arab cultures as well. The historic *caravansarais* (inns for travelers) of the Islamic world, especially along the Silk Road, gave merchants and others lodging, safety, and food. They offered hospitality without charging and recouped costs by levying a tax on all trading done within the safety of the inn walls. Many cultures throughout history have shared the conviction that one must provide food, shelter, and safety without cost to the stranger.

Hospitality is still a deeply held value in different cultures today. Examples range from the Pashtun in Afghanistan, whose honor code demands offering protection even to an enemy who requests it, to the Bantu-inhabited regions of East Africa, where sharing food and home with others underscores the importance of brotherhood and sisterhood. Hospitality is offered even outside homes, as in Japanese cities where friends and acquaintances meet in public spaces, restaurants, and tea/

coffee shops, or in Nepal where locals offered tea to foreigners after the 2015 earthquake, boiling water amid the rubble of their lost homes.

Hospitality understood as providing food, shelter, and safety is a strong thread in Christian traditions as well. The Old Testament commands us to welcome strangers (Leviticus 19:33-34). The New Testament church was known for how its members cared for one another (Acts 2:44-45). Indeed, Jesus calls us to love our neighbor as ourselves (Matthew 25:40 and Mark 12:31), and Paul echoes Jesus' teaching to be a good neighbor and practice hospitality (Romans 12; 15:2; Galatians 5:14). Jesus even describes caring for others, including welcoming strangers, as worthy of heavenly reward (Matthew 25:37-45). Showing hospitality is part of a transformed Christian life as described by Paul in Romans 12:13: "Share with the Lord's people who are in need. Practice hospitality." In this passage, the word *hospitality* is a common translation of the Greek word *philoxenia*—the love of strangers. You might recognize pieces of this Greek word in *Philadelphia*, the city of brotherly love, and *xenophobia*, the fear of strangers. Curiously in English we still have the word for fearing strangers but have lost the word for loving them.

LOVE YOUR NEIGHBOR

As hard as it may be, we are called to act with kindness and extend love not only to brothers, sisters, and strangers but also to enemies (Matthew 5:43-48), providing them food and water when needed (Proverbs 25:21-22; Luke 6:27-28; Romans 12:20). The good neighbor from whom we might accept help or to whom we give help may even be an enemy of our people, as in the story of the Good Samaritan (Luke 10:25-37).

If we can value hospitality and affirm the command to love neighbors—friends, strangers, *and* enemies—what prevents us from doing so? For many, selfishness and fear get in the way. If we are honest, we can admit that we would rather do what is comfortable. We don't want strangers cramping our style or threatening our secure sense of how the world works. As hosts, we might feel that our home isn't big enough or nice enough or clean enough. As guests, we don't want to seem pushy or needy. As enemies, we see no reason "to do that for her after what she did to him." "Anyway," our arguing continues, "there are risks involved, and I don"t have time." Such are our surface excuses for not prioritizing hospitality and loving our neighbor. We may trivialize the call to hospitality by reducing it to logistics.

We can also avoid being hospitable out of a deeper fear of losing our own identity or place in the world. Psychologists, sociologists, and philosophers suggest that we define ourselves in part in opposition to others: what we are *not* helps us understand what we are. In defining ourselves and creating community, we commonly exclude the other. Exclusion can be physical but also emotional, political, and social. It is not just the mean people who exclude others.

Despite the inconveniences or even the risks of showing hospitality, we cannot ignore God's call to love our neighbor. Extending kindness and welcome is not optional for Christians. Hospitality is not primarily a duty of extroverts with large homes but extends more broadly to how we relate to others. With this in mind, hospitality becomes a way of living with others who are different, not just an event on the calendar.

EMBRACING OTHERS

When the COEXIST bumper stickers (the C a sickle, the X a star of David, and the T a Christian cross) first came out, I liked the idea that members of world religions might be able to relate to one another without the need to detonate bombs. As the meme grew popular, I noticed variations: the symbols for O, E, I, and S were swapped out for symbols of peace, Buddhism, Wicca, gender inclusivity, science, paganism, and superman, among others. The more variations I saw, the more uncomfortable I felt with the idea of "COEXIST."

When we coexist and there is no open conflict, we can believe we are listening to each other and being hospitable. But in fact this type of tolerance often allows us to remain ignorant of others' beliefs and perspectives and to avoid difficult conversations. Willful ignorance is a type of exclusion. I might coexist with people who are different from me, but that does not mean I have extended hospitality to them, either of the food-welcome-shelter or of the open-my-heart variety. A COEXIST mantra allows me to go my own way, a way described by contemporary Christian theologian Miroslav Volf as "a civilized form of exclusion." If we exclude everyone who is different from us by just "letting them be," we cannot learn from them. We cannot grow, and we cannot truly understand ourselves.

Volf wrote his important work *Exclusion and Embrace* out of his experiences as a Croatian after the war in the former Yugoslavia. In his theology of embrace, he was looking for how to work together toward truth and justice in light of past conflicts and future togetherness. Far riskier than inviting your neighbor for tea, embrace involves inviting your neighbor or your enemy into your heart. That is the essence of a bigger hospitality. Volf understands embrace as involving four steps, as we learn to extend this bigger hospitality.

In Step 1, we open our arms to show a desire for and openness to the other. Open arms are an invitation, and they signal an open heart and mind. We must open our mind and heart to listen to others, to hear their stories from their own lips. We must not just tune in to the summaries of what they said as provided by the pundits we like most. Other people need to know that we are trying to open our heart and mind to listen to them.

Then in Step 2, we wait. We do not force an encounter

on our terms and only on our turf. This can be a scary decision. If we invite strangers into our home or our life, they may make us uncomfortable, cost time and money, or reject us. If we listen with care to the ideas and perspectives of others, they may confuse us or challenge what we believe and who we are. Yet desire to love our neighbors keeps our arms open, waiting. If they do not immediately move toward us, we still wait. If they reject us, we continue to wait with our arms open.

Step 3 happens when the other person enters our open arms. It is represented by a closing of arms in a mutual embrace. This embrace expresses respect rooted in the love of neighbor as self. Each person mirrors the other—the goal is not for one to dominate. We welcome each other to a sharing of ourselves—a bigger hospitality.

In Step 4, our arms open again. The other person is not conquered but allowed to withdraw. Perhaps neither she nor I will give up our convictions, but we release the other person in hope. This creates space for future encounters, allowing us to continue to connect with one another despite our differences. Each person lives with the memory of being drawn into embrace, of tuning in briefly to the voice and presence of another in a common space.

This powerful theological metaphor of embrace embodies an attitude of hospitality toward others that goes beyond offering food and shelter. This hospitality becomes a way of living in the world and living with one another. It embodies a type of peace-making. Indeed, it is rooted in the grace with which God has embraced us. In the story of the two brothers, told by Jesus in Luke 15:11-32, the loving father allows his younger son to take his inheritance and go into a far country. But when the younger son comes to his senses and returns home ready to take up the role of a stranger and servant, the father welcomes him with open arms. "But while he was still a long way off," Jesus tells us, "his father saw him and was filled with compassion for him; he ran to his son, threw his arms around him and kissed him" (Luke 15:20). The younger son basks in his father's embrace, but the father also keeps his arms open to receive the petulant older son who envies his brother's welcome. To this son the father says, "you are always with me, and everything I have is yours," while gently inviting him to join in the communal embrace (Luke 15:31). God's embrace of each of us calls us to embrace one another.

Volf's understanding of embrace is radically different from a COEXIST-ent tolerating of each other. His embrace—this bigger hospitality—represents welcoming the stranger and listening well to others. Embrace comes out of the Christian conviction that love is the needed response to people whoever they are. Embrace does not mean I have to sacrifice my convictions. We can strongly hold to certain beliefs and pieces of our identity. But the commitment to listen, and the memory of ourselves as differently shaped during the embrace, can create a more hospitable self. Practicing this bigger hospitality can help us understand better who we are, what we believe, and why we believe it.

Sometimes headlines of racial tensions, terrorist attacks, protests in Ukraine, Hong Kong, Phnom Penh, or Ferguson and Baltimore leave little hope for peace. Being too busy, lazy, or scared to invite a neighbor for coffee does *not* somehow result directly in race riots. But unless we in our communities, as families and individuals, seek to embrace people who are different from us in our lives and world—creating space to hear their voices, learning to show hospitality in its broadest sense, overcoming our fears, and being open to possibly changing our shape to enable embrace—we cannot become a welcoming place for each other. We will then live in unwelcoming, fractured, and possibly warring communities.

An attitude of embrace—a bigger hospitality—offers hope for our future together. Being willing to open the doors of our home and church to people who are different from us is the beginning. The willingness to let others in or to meet others in their spaces, to share a meal, and to listen well places cultural differences in the context of love of neighbor and love of God.

This image of someone standing at the door waiting to be invited in echoes Revelation 3:20, where Jesus waits to be welcomed by his busy and careless followers. If they pause to listen, if they repent, believe, and open the door, he will enter and eat with them—and with us. We see the fruits of hospitality in the story of Jesus appearing after his resurrection to the two disciples on the road to Emmaus (Luke 24:13-35). As they near the village, they invite Jesus to join them for dinner, *and* they are open to listening to him. In these acts of hospitality, they see truth and receive grace, like others in Scripture who found that God can come to us in the guise of a stranger.

Loving our neighbor by showing both traditional hospitality and a bigger attitude of hospitality is not a trivial matter. Opening our doors, sharing what we have, and listening with our hearts connect intercultural learning with love of God and neighbor.

7

Engaging
with Grace

Intercultural communication and practices have been part of the Christian tradition from its very beginning. As we saw in Chapter Two, the early church was made up of people from a variety of cultures. The mission impulse in Christianity, the desire to spread the gospel, encouraged faithful Christians to move beyond their cultures into other parts of the world. Sometimes these moves were good: Christian churches are now present around the globe. Other times, this movement into other cultures had horrible effects, as we see in the medieval crusades or in the removal of indigenous children from their mothers, homes, and cultures in the US and other countries.

Today more than ever, we all find ourselves in intercultural situations. The growth of international travel and business are obvious reasons, but there are cultural differences within the borders of our countries, cities, and neighborhoods. Just down the road, you may find a group of people who share a language, religion, customs, and stories that shape their identities in ways very different from your own. While it was once possible to stay in our own valley, as described in Chapter One, the contemporary world brings new people and perspectives into communities and workplaces, congregations and schools, living rooms and twitter feeds.

Race and ethnicities form part of our cultural backgrounds. We are shaped by experiences that are related to the color of our skin, the way we dress, or the religious beliefs we hold dear. When people not only have different beliefs and practices but also look different, the lines of cultural differences are often more sharply drawn. Headlines from Eastern Europe, South Africa, Jerusalem, the US, and many other areas highlight the challenges faced by people who share the same geographic space but identify themselves in very different cultural ways that are tied to racial and ethnic experiences. When these different groups fail to engage interculturally in smart ways, the results can be disastrous and even fatal.

What role can Christians play in this muddy world of cultural clashes and misunderstandings? In Chapter Six, we suggested that living out the theological metaphor of embrace can become a kind of peace-making. We can be peacemakers, a type of person our world desperately needs. We can be peacemakers because we value in all humans the image of God and because we see cultural diversity as a part of God's creative genius and our creative nature. We can be peacemakers as a response to biblical calls to be peace-loving and "to sow in peace" (James 3:17-18).

At the same time, we understand the need to sift both our own culture and other cultures for wisdom and goodness. We do not accept everything that our own or another culture has packaged together because none of us and none of our cultures are perfect. We can draw on the strong traditions of hospitality found throughout the world and add our Christian callings to love our neighbors and our enemies. In our grace-inspired hopes of being able to love both neighbors and enemies, we can work to open our hearts to those whose traditions, perspectives, and histories are different from our own.

INTERCULTURAL LEARNING

Several frameworks and many books and training tools have been developed to help us engage effectively with people who have been formed in other cultures. Such practical frameworks can help us bridge the larger task of becoming the kind of person who can love our neighbor and the concrete skills and understanding that can be ingredients in that growth. A focus on skills alone risks losing the big-picture connections to grace, love, and justice that give meaning and motivation to intercultural learning. A focus on opening our hearts alone can leave us well-intentioned but clumsy and inept. We need frameworks that will help us learn in specific ways to connect vision and practice. The various approaches each define in their own way which skills to focus on, and many offer training materials, trainer certification seminars, and assessment programs. When we want to get better at intercultural learning, understanding, and just plain getting along with others, developing a framework from these different approaches can help us.

Let's consider three kinds of learning that can improve our ability to engage interculturally:

- gaining *knowledge* about other cultures, ourselves, and intercultural engagement;
- interpreting *cultural practices and motivations*;
- improving *interpersonal skills* that shape how we engage.

GAINING KNOWLEDGE ABOUT CULTURES, OURSELVES, AND INTERCULTURAL ENGAGEMENT

Knowledge about ourselves and others helps us get a clearer picture of both. To understand and interact in good ways with other people, it is important to know about the customs and core beliefs as well as the specific histories that form a culture or people group, including our own. As a faculty member, I have led groups of students on study trips to learn about development work in Southeast Asia, particularly Cambodia. Most of the students know very little about Cambodia, and they have no memories of the Viet Nam War and its effects in that region of the world. One of their mandatory assignments prior to departure is to learn some of the facts and listen to some of the stories of the Cambodian Holocaust. Learning about the devastation of the Khmer Rouge years (1975-79) and its effects on the economy, cities, society, and almost every family in the country is a necessary foundation for understanding the current social, political, and development issues.

This assignment might seem like a no-brainer. Of course, you have to learn about the biggest, most horrible recent national experience in order to understand a country and people today. However, the same holds true for other people we may wish to engage, even when they are not half a world away. We should build our knowledge about groups of people who are relatively new to our community. We can explore their traditions, perspectives, history, and group experiences through appropriate films and books and by inviting them to share their stories. If people who look different, talk different, and act different live down the street, we should invite them over for coffee and share our histories and personal stories. To pretend that they live in a different universe is to practice a form of exclusion, as Miroslav Volf reminded us in Chapter Six.

If our congregation hopes to reach out to a neighborhood, we should build our knowledge about the economics, demographics, and worship preferences of those who live in that community. We can do good research, and we can also ask neighborhood residents to tell us their stories. If we are disturbed or saddened, angry or outraged at the race-related news events coming out of the Middle East, Europe, and the US, we should take a step toward understanding by digging beyond the headlines. We should build our knowledge of others, the facts, their stories, and their perspectives that are different from our own and from those of our favorite commentators.

Another piece for building our knowledge is understanding how our own culture shapes us, what our biases or preferences are and why we have them. My son once asked if I was stressed at work. This question seemed to come out of the blue, so I wondered what made him ask. "Well," he paused. "You've been cooking a lot of rice for dinner. Rice is your comfort food, so I figure you must need to eat rice." I hadn't been thinking that I needed to eat rice, but my son was right: work had been particularly stressful. He was tuned in to my personal biases or preferences more than I was. (The fact that he was longing for mashed potatoes was beside the point!)

The insight here is that we all have biases or preferences, many of which lie just beneath our sightline. These biases affect what we do, why we do things, and how we think. They are part of our identity. In many cases, they are shaped by the culture in which we grew up. When we become more aware of how our culture has shaped who we are, we are better able to see cultural misunderstandings and differences for what they are. We can consider another way of acting or another perspective as potentially reasonable inside another cultural context and not necessarily as dumb or wrong.

A third piece for building our knowledge is learning about the challenges as well as the benefits of engaging with people from other cultures who are different from us. Learning about the challenges can help us overcome fears and be willing to adjust our expectations when we encounter new experiences. On a recent study trip to Cambodia that I co-directed, students visited the Cheoung Ek Genocidal Center near Phnom Penh, the site of one of the infamous "killing fields." The memorial park at Cheoung Ek features a Buddhist stupa, an acrylic-sided monument filled with over 5,000 human skulls. Touring this site was a difficult experience for middle-class students from the US. One of them wrote,

> As I walked around the memorial … one of the skulls caught my eye. This skull had no distinguishing feature, but when I saw it my mind created the living person who once had this skull in their head. I could see this person eating, laughing, and talking to people, experiencing similar hopes and fears that I feel. This person could have been me, a normal, law-abiding citizen. My skull could be staring blankly out of a glass box at somber tourists seeing hundreds of skulls just like mine. But I stand on the other side of the glass. This person happened to be at the wrong place at the wrong time while I happened to be born at a better place at a better time. This determined which

side of the glass I looked through in the Memorial Stupa. I have done nothing to deserve the life I have.

Before we visited Cheoung Ek, I had asked my students to think about this question, "As a result of learning about Cambodia, what new pieces have been added to your picture of God's world?" I wanted them to not just report what they had seen, but also to adjust the way they understood their own lives and the lives of others. Although visiting Cheoung Ek was a difficult experience, this encounter with the stories and physical remains of other people expanded the students' knowledge of the world and their empathy for others, and it gave them a new perspective on their own lives.

INTERPRETING CULTURAL PRACTICES AND MOTIVATIONS

In addition to knowing our own culture better and learning about the history and culture of other people, we also need to acquire the habit of interpreting cultural practices, the specific behaviors involved in them, and their motivations. When we learn *why* people *do* certain things, we are learning about both their practices and their motivations. Rather than simply thinking that people are acting inappropriately or weirdly, we can then begin to understand their behaviors and practices. All cultures have specific rules for all kinds of things related to behavior, including speaking styles, personal space, and hand gestures, and these are linked to important interpersonal courtesies such as showing respect, hospitality, and appreciation.

For instance in mainstream white US-America, when someone is talking to us, we make eye contact. Catching someone's eye and holding their gaze shows that we are listening. If we look out the window or watch a fly in the room, the speaker might assume we are distracted or bored. If we stare at the ground, we might be dishonest or hiding something. In some other cultures, both within the US and abroad, the appropriate behavior when someone, especially a superior, is speaking to you is to avoid prolonged eye contact. Holding the speaker's gaze too long shows disrespect.

Specific behaviors join up to create stable cultural practices that involve matters such as showing respect, greeting or leave-taking, or eating together. However, the same behaviors can have different meanings in different locations. For example if you are traveling to Asia, you might be told *not* to scrape your plate clean at the end of the meal. Leaving a small amount shows your host that you have been given more than enough food and do not wish to have your plate refilled. But this practice is not that simple. Leaving food on your plate in China is a compliment to your host: he has fed you well. The same behavior in Thailand, however, indicates that you are wealthy: you have no need to finish all your food. So leaving food on your plate can be interpreted as showing off that you are a rich American traveling in a poor country. Meanwhile not eating all the food on your plate in Cambodia is considered bad manners because it is so wasteful. In other words, leaving food on your plate in different Asian cultures can be interpreted in different ways, from being a compliment to a sign of social status to bad manners. A tour book for Asia might recommend in a list of "do's & don'ts" that you leave food on your plate. But a simple list of behaviors without some understanding of the deeper values, motivations, and perspectives and of how they give meaning to cultural practices can lead to misunderstandings.

Taking time to learn these deeper values, and setting aside our own biases and prejudices to do so, is important if we are to understand the behaviors and cultural practices of other people. When I lived in New Zealand, I visited a Maori cultural center. The Maori are the indigenous people of the New Zealand islands. When we were invited into their meeting house, the village representatives were seated facing to the right. We, the visitors, took seats opposite them facing to the left. The men were invited to sit in the front, while women were directed to the back. I was disappointed because this separated me from the rest of my family, and I couldn't see up front very well. Nevertheless, I did what I was told. I didn't want to draw attention to myself, but also I knew that I was a guest in someone else's house of worship. I wanted to respect the house rules. I wanted to be a good guest. But I assumed that this cultural practice of segregating the women from the men placed women in a lesser position.

From the back row, I listened as our host, Tom, explain

what had just happened. The seating arrangement, a Maori custom, was not because the women were less valued. Traditionally, the men were seated closest to the hosting villagers because that protected the women from possible danger. Contrary to my assumptions, the seating arrangement showed special honor (not less) to the women in the house. Tom was aware of how other cultures might interpret the Maori seating customs, and he wanted to bridge the gap. By explaining, he helped the guests understand what was happening and why, to see the history behind the tradition, and to appreciate the honor being shown to the women. Not only did he explain the motivation behind the Maori practice of seating men and women in different places, but he also displayed true intercultural learning by recognizing that those from other cultures might understand this practice in a different way. He wanted to give us a glimpse into Maori culture and to enable us to understand a set of behaviors from within their cultural context. I needed the combination of cultural knowledge about practices, values, and perspectives in order to interpret the motivations and this particular practice in the right way.

Looking people in the eye, or not; leaving food on your plate, or not; seating men and women separately, or not—these are three examples of differing cultural practices that are reasonably motivated within their cultural contexts.

As we pay attention to different cultural practices and the motivations behind them, we learn about our own assumptions, the ways we tend to behave, and why we behave these ways, which we had perhaps never noticed before. We also learn to appreciate why other people are different from us. Paying attention to behaviors, cultural practices, and motivations helps us when we travel but also when we are the hosts. If we want to create a welcoming place for others in our home, church, and community, we need to create spaces where we don't all need to look the same, eat the same, or sit in the same way.

IMPROVING INTERPERSONAL SKILLS

Understanding the cultural practices and motivations of other people might seem to be a big task—too big in a world as diverse as ours. But as cross-cultural expert David Livermore has pointed out, learning all the rules of all the cultures we encounter is not the goal. Instead, we want to learn a set of skills that will help us become more observant, open, and flexible as we engage with others.

In Chapter Five, we talked about the fact that good intentions are not enough. But they are certainly a good place to begin. If we want to relate well to people whose culture is different from our own, then we will seek to develop the skills that will help us better interact with them. Perhaps we will take a class to improve our communication skills. Perhaps we will practice becoming a better listener—sitting to the side of a group discussion and paying attention to what each person is saying, the gestures one uses, the pauses another makes. Perhaps we will take note of how many questions we ask at the dinner table—and how well we listen to the answers—and compare this observation to the amount of time we spend talking about ourselves. If we don't take the time to be with people—to "waste" time by simply being alert and attentive in their presence—we will not develop the interpersonal skills we need to engage in intercultural learning.

One student studying in Beijing made this important discovery for herself:

> I think one reason I find studying Chinese so attractive is the people I have met. . . . It is one thing to read about Chinese culture and another thing to have hours of conversation with my conversation partners about how they view marriage, government reforms, and methods of teaching English. However much information I can glean from reading, I find I care about something so much more when a friend is telling me about it.

This student learned that taking the time to make a friend from a different culture gave her both a friend and a way to better understand that friend's way of life.

Observation skills and attentiveness can help us notice and be tuned in to the social and emotional dynamics of a situation. Openness to others and their perspectives and the ability to empathize can help us be more winsome as we gain insights into why people do what they do. Flexibility keeps us from over-reacting and allows us the social and relational space to discern, for example, what is the wisest course of action as opposed to what seems normal or easiest to us. Working on specific behavioral skills—like remembering to accept gifts with both hands or to shake hands or to avoid staring—helps us to interact with others in ways that they are able to receive as respectful. Likewise working on interpersonal skills as part of our intercultural capabilities will have positive spill over into all our relationships as we practice understanding people and as we continue learning about others, their perspectives, and their lives.

GROWING IN GRACE

Building our intercultural capabilities is not this year's ministry focus, and next year we move on to something else. Improving how we work with and understand others—those who are a bit different from us and those who are really different from us—is a life-long journey. Here's the good news: we can educate ourselves and raise the children in our church and those around our dinner table to be more interculturally capable, to live more gracefully with others. We *can* make a difference as we improve our abilities as individuals, families, and Christians in communities to act and react in better ways across the lines of our fractured world. We can indeed become peacemakers in a world longing for shalom.

8

Encouragement

Throughout this book, we have seen that Christian identity and intercultural learning fundamentally belong together. God created us in his own creative image. As we saw in Chapter Two, wise culture building happens when we shape our surroundings by crafting tools, words, dwellings, images, and practices that enable delight in God, delight in creation, and delight in other people. Yet our culture building will be different from the culture building in the next valley, country, and continent. And because both we and they travel, immigrate, and settle down in new places, we will often find ourselves living next to those whom we are called to love as neighbors but whose culture we find baffling and perhaps even scary.

At the same time, engaging with people and ideas that are different from our own offers us opportunities to learn. Bill Nye the Science Guy, speaking to a class of college graduates, commented: "Everyone you will ever meet knows something you don't." When we explore the literature, music, customs, language, traditions, and stories of other people and cultures, we can discover pieces of God's creation, insights about the world, and lessons for life. As we try to understand the beliefs and practices of others from their perspective, we begin to consider how our own ways are similar and different. We can reflect on which pieces of our cultures and identities are absolutely essential and which we can be flexible about. We can improve our intercultural skills and grow into more thoughtful, empathetic, and discerning people. In fact, looking for reflections of the Creator in other cultures can be part of figuring out what is good and what needs to be changed in our own life and culture.

Cultural differences are part of the world we live in. We will encounter people, cultures, and ideas that are different from our own. What might happen if we approached our intercultural encounters as opportunities to learn from others and about ourselves? What if we tried to embrace the stranger, the foreigner, and even the enemy? As Miroslav Volf reminds us, *embrace* does not mean accepting everything we encounter. But we can make space in our heart and mind to see from other perspectives and to hear other stories. We can learn from others. Perhaps we can grow more flexible in how we act. Maybe we'll gain a greater appreciation for our own core beliefs. We might even see God in a new way.

Jamie learned this lesson when a newcomer sat next to him on a Sunday morning. During the singing, the stranger raised his hands in praise—not something Jamie grew up with. Jamie was not bothered by the stranger who praised God in this way, but he did not feel the need to raise his hands himself. Then to his surprise, Jamie's young son Eli, watching the neighbor in his pew, slowly raised his three-year-old hands in praise. In the next moment, Jamie stepped over the hurdle of his own cultural preferences.

For the sake of his son, Jamie lifted his hands, too. He wanted Eli to know it is okay to worship in different ways. In that simple gesture, Jamie created a welcoming place for the stranger in his pew, and he experienced—for the first time in his life—a different way of praising God.

WHY WE NEED OTHERS

We have much to learn about God from people whose ways are different from our own. In 1996, the Lutheran World Federation drafted *The Nairobi Statement on Worship and Culture*. This statement elegantly summarizes how Christian worship is contextual, intercultural, counter-cultural, and transcultural. Worship practices arise in cultural contexts, so worship is always contextual, a particular way of meeting God in a particular time and particular place. At the same time, elements of Christian worship can be shared interculturally across different settings around the world. Christian worship thus can be transformative, prompting us to discern the good in different cultural practices. But Christian worship also directs our attention away from ourselves toward God, and in doing so, it urges us toward confession and repentance. Worship is counter-cultural; it is intended to make us look critically at our familiar, everyday lives. And Christian worship focuses on the resurrected Christ who transcends all cultures.

The Nairobi Statement reminds us that Christian worship itself demands from us a certain level of intercultural learning. There are many good and various ways to worship and know God. Seeking out other experiences of Christian worship or other ways of seeing the world are not necessarily a rejection of one's own culture and ideas. But as in the example of the Afghan women in Chapter Three who because of their cultural background can help Western readers see the woman at the well with different eyes, we have much to gain from other Christians.

In Paul's description of the church as one body with many parts (1 Corinthians 12), we see our need for others who are different from us. A spun yarn of one fiber type can be used to knit a fabric, but 100% alpaca, though incredibly soft, will tend to stretch and loose shape. Pure wool can provide warmth when wet but can be scratchy. Possum or cashmere or angora give fluff and insulation but tend to be weak and shed a lot of hair. My favorite yarns are the blends: possum or cashmere for loft spun with wool for resilience and perhaps a touch of silk for luster and strength. These favorite blends bring the best that each fiber has to offer into a garment that will last. The diversity that can make us uncomfortable or even scared can also make us stronger, more resilient, and possibly more useful in the world.

As we learn to practice a wider hospitality—to embrace the stranger and be embraced in turn—and as we do this *because* we are Christians, we will find ourselves living out the Great Commandment: to love God with all our heart and soul and mind, and to love our neighbor as ourselves

(Matthew 22:36-40). We will find that we are not standing apart, as the older brother in the parable did, judging both his younger brother and his father. Instead, we will find ourselves enveloped in the Father's open arms, pressed close to his heart and to the brothers and sisters he welcomes home.

Notes

Series Editor's Foreword

7 **Midway along the journey of my life:** the opening verse of *The Inferno* by Dante Alighieri, trans. Mark Musa (Bloomington and Indianapolis: Indiana University Press, 1995), 19.

8 **We are always on the road:** from Calvin's 34th sermon on Deuteronomy (5:12-14), preached on June 20, 1555 (*Ioannis Calvini Opera quae supersunt Omnia*, ed. Johann-Wilhelm Baum et al. [Brunsvigae: C.A. Schwetschke et Filium, 1883], 26.291), as quoted by Herman Selderhuis (*John Calvin: A Pilgrim's Life* [Downers Grove, IL: InterVarsity, 2009], 34).

8 **a gift of divine kindness:** from the last chapter of Calvin's French version of the *Institutes of the Christian Religion*. Titled "Of the Christian Life," the entire chapter is a guide to wise and faithful living in this world. (*John Calvin, Institutes of the Christian Religion, 1541 French Edition*, trans. Elsie Anne McKee [Grand Rapids: Eerdmans, 2009], 704.)

Chapter 1

14 **It may surprise us to find that the word *culture* originally meant tilling the land:** Terry Eagleton, *The Idea of Culture* (Oxford: Wiley-Blackwell, 2000), 1-2.

14 **For those who want to dig a little deeper:** Some other books that dig further into various aspects of this topic include: E. Randolph

Richards & Brandon J. O'Brien, *Misreading Scripture with Western Eyes: Removing Cultural Blinders to Better Understand the Bible* (Downers Grove, IL: InterVarsity Press, 2012); Philip Jenkins, *The New Faces of Christianity: Believing the Bible in the Global South* (New York: Oxford University Press, 2006); David I. Smith, *Learning from the Stranger: Christian Faith and Cultural Diversity* (Grand Rapids: Eerdmans, 2009); Andrew F. Walls, *The Cross-Cultural Process in Christian History: Studies in the Transmission and Appropriation of Faith* (Maryknoll, NY: Orbis, 2002); David Livermore, *Cultural Intelligence: Improving Your CQ to Engage Our Multicultural World* (Grand Rapids: Baker Academic, 2009).

Chapter 2

21 **Ancient Greece split the world:** See, for example, R. H. Robins, *A Short History of Linguistics* (London: Longman, 1979), 11.

21 **Natives of Papua New Guinea suspected at first:** See Mitchell Zuckoff, *Lost in Shangri-La: A True Story of Survival, Adventure, and the Most Incredible Rescue Mission of World War II* (New York: HarperCollins, 2011), 186-89.

21 **saw their rulers as "images" or representatives of their gods:** On the image of God, see J. Richard Middleton, *The Liberating Image: The Imago Dei in Genesis 1* (Grand Rapids: Brazos, 2005).

23 **A recent study of the automatic brain responses of Americans and Japanese:** J. Y. Chiao et al., "Cultural Specificity in Amygdala Response to Fear Faces," *Journal of Cognitive Neuroscience* 20 (2008): 2167-74.

24 **God did not make others as I would have made them:** Dietrich Bonhoeffer, *Life Together and Prayerbook of the Bible. Dietrich Bonhoeffer Works, Volume 5*, trans. D. W. Bloesch and J. H. Burtness (Minneapolis: Fortress Press, 1996), 95.

25 **One study tells the story of an older Korean woman:** Paja Lee Donnelly, "Ethics and Cross-Cultural Nursing," *Journal of Transcultural Nursing* 11, no. 2 (2000): 119-26.

28 **Jerusalem was made up of both Greek and Aramaic speakers:**
David A. Fiensy, "The Composition of the Jerusalem Church," in *The Book of Acts in its First Century Setting*, Vol. 4, ed. Richard Bauckham (Grand Rapids: Eerdmans; Carlisle: Paternoster, 1995), 213-36.

30 **The Ephesian metaphors of the temple and of the body:** Andrew F. Walls, *The Cross-Cultural Process in Christian History* (Maryknoll, NY, Edinburgh: Orbis, T&T Clark, 2002), 79, alluding to Ephesians 4:13.

Chapter 3

34 *Though not a prostitute…. His obvious wish to reform her life …:* These words are drawn from various Bible commentaries on John.

34 **Psychologists have studied how people in different cultures explain events:** See for example Incheol Choi, Richard E. Nisbett, and Ara Norenzayan, "Causal attribution across cultures: Variation and universality," *Psychological Bulletin*, 125, no. 1 (1999): 47-63.

35 **I recently ran across this passage in Kate McCord:** Kate McCord, *In the Land of Blue Burqas* (Chicago: Moody Publishers, 2012), 305. Kate McCord is a pseudonym.

Chapter 4

41 **German watchmaker named Johannes Emde:** Stephen Neill, *A History of Christian Missions* (Harmondsworth: Penguin, 1986), 246.

44 **chatting with some English-speaking teens:** David I. Smith, *Learning from the Stranger: Christian Faith and Cultural Difference* (Grand Rapids: Eerdmans, 2009), 1-4.

45 **the most striking feature of Christianity at the beginning of the third millennium:** Andrew F. Walls, "Eusebius Tries Again: The Task of Reconceiving and Re-visioning the Study of Christian History," in *Enlarging the Story: Perspectives on Writing World Christian History,* ed. Wilbert R. Shenk (Maryknoll, NY: Orbis Books, 2002), 11.

47 **In the past few decades, various popular books:** See, for example, Sherwood G. Lingenfelter and Marvin K. Mayers, *Ministering*

Cross-culturally: An Incarnational Model for Personal Relationships, 2nd ed. (Grand Rapids: Baker Academic, 2003); Duane Elmer, Cross-Cultural Servanthood: Serving the World in Christlike Humility (Downers Grove, IL: InterVarsity Press, 2006). The most recent edition of Lingenfelter and Mayers' text drops the incarnational language, providing an example of its decline: Sherwood G. Lingenfelter and Marvin K. Mayers, Ministering Cross-Culturally: A Model for Effective Personal Relationships, 3rd ed. (Grand Rapids: Baker Academic, 2016).

48 **Some have implied that what Jesus was doing in the incarnation was itself intercultural learning:** See, for example, Lingenfelter and Mayers (2nd ed.), 22-25.

Chapter 5

53 **Minh settled in easily**: Minh is a pseudonym.

Chapter 6

60 **In the Papyrus of Ani, a text from ancient Egypt:** Kevin O'Gorman, "The Origins of Hospitality. Inaugural Lecture," Online video, YouTube, 28 January 2015, Web accessed 20 October 2015. https://www.youtube.com/watch?v=6oDBaAC65HM

64 **described by contemporary Christian theologian Miroslav Volf as "a civilized form of exclusion":** Miroslav Volf, "Exclusion and Embrace: Theological Reflections in the Wake of 'Ethnic Cleansing,'" in Emerging Voices in Global Christian Theology, ed. William A. Dyrness (Grand Rapids: Zondervan 1994), 19-46.

64 **Volf wrote his important work *Exclusion and Embrace*:** Miroslav Volf, Exclusion and Embrace: A Theological Exploration of Identity, Otherness, and Reconciliation (Nashville: Abingdon Press, 1996).

Chapter 7

75 **Learning about the devastation of the Khmer Rouge years:** See for example Theary C. Seng, Daughter of the Killing Fields: Asrei's Story

(London: Fusion Press, 2005); John Pilger, "Year Zero—The Silent Death of Cambodia [1979]," online video, *YouTube*, 24 February 2013, Web accessed 20 October 2015, http://johnpilger.com/videos/year-zero-the-silent-death-of-cambodia; and Joel Brinkley, *Cambodia's Curse: The Modern History of a Troubled Land* (New York: Public Affairs, 2011).

77 **On a recent study trip to Cambodia**: This student reflection is included in Donald G. DeGraaf, *There and Back: Living and Learning Abroad* (Grand Rapids: Calvin College Press, 2015), 117-118.

82 **But as cross-cultural expert David Livermore has pointed out:** David Livermore, *Serving with Eyes Wide Open* (Grand Rapids: Baker Books, 2006); David Livermore, "Leading with Cultural Intelligence," online video, *YouTube*, 24 September 2009, Web accessed 21 October 2015, https://www.youtube.com/watch?v=SMi7yhHjASQ.

83 **One student studying in Beijing**: This student reflection is included in DeGraaf, *There and Back*, 72.

Chapter 8

87 **Bill Nye the Science Guy, speaking to a class of college graduates:** Alexandra Vokos, "Bill Nye tells Rutgers Grads: We are 'Much More Alike Than Different,'" *Huffington Post*, 20 May 2015, Web accessed 20 October 2015, http://www.huffingtonpost.com/2015/05/20/bill-nye-rutgers-commencement_n_7338214.html.

89 ***The Nairobi Statement on Worship and Culture*:** To read the full text visit: http://worship.calvin.edu/resources/resource-library/nairobi-statement-on-worship-and-culture-full-text (Web accessed 21 October 2015). *The Nairobi Statement* uses the word "cross-cultural" for what we call "intercultural" in this book.